When I caught my first glimpse of the country

ch I descended, my heart fell like a stone.

Deserts
of the Heart

Finding God during the Dry Times

PAMELA REEVE

Multnomah®Publishers *Sisters, Oregon*

DESERTS OF THE HEART
published by Multnomah Publishers, Inc.

© 2000 by Pamela Reeve
International Standard Book Number: 1-57673-436-6

Cover photography by © John MacMurray Jr.

Unless otherwise noted, Scripture quotations are from:
The Holy Bible, New International Version
©1973, 1984 by International Bible Society,
used by permission of Zondervan Publishing House

Also quoted:
The Holy Bible, New King James Version (NKJV)
© 1984 by Thomas Nelson, Inc.

New American Standard Bible (NASB)
© 1960, 1977 by the Lockman Foundation

The Living Bible (TLB)
© 1971. Used by permission of Tyndale House Publishers, Inc.
All rights reserved.

Multnomah is a trademark of Multnomah Publishers, Inc.
and is registered in the U.S. Patent and Trademark Office.
The colophon is a trademark of Multnomah Publishers, Inc.

For information:
Multnomah Publishers, Inc.
Post Office Box 1720
Sisters, Oregon 97759

Library of Congress Cataloging-in-Publication Data

Reeve, Pamela.
   Deserts of the Heart : Finding God During the Dry Times / by Pamela Reeve.
      p. cm.
   ISBN 1-57673-436-6
   1. Spiritual life—Christianity. 2. Reeve, Pamela. 3.
Deserts—Religious aspects—Christianity. I. Title.
   BV4501.2 .R4238 2000
   248.8'6--dc21
                                                    00-010594

00 01 02 03 04 05 06 07 08 — 10 9 8 7 6 5 4 3 2 1 0

To the memory of Amy Carmichael,
who awakened my heart to the joy
of knowing Christ as the Beloved.

He opened my eyes to see
a well in the desert—
a gushing spring in the midst
of hopeless desolation.

Contents

ACKNOWLEDGMENTS

For many years I had thought about writing this book. Don Jacobson, Multnomah's president and publisher, empowered me to do it with his ability to inspire and his warm support. His commitment to demonstrating Christian principles in the publishing world makes it a joy to be associated with the Multnomah Publishers team that he leads.

For twenty-one years, Larry Libby has edited my books. With his ability to give life to leaden text, he has been God's gift to me. Even more than his artistry with words, I have appreciated the oneness of mind we have had. Only Larry would have borne with me through my twenty-two revisions. This is really more our book than my book. I am deeply indebted to him.

Working with Multnomah's very creative designer, Stephen Gardner, has been an experience beyond my expectations. His goal all the way through has been to visualize the text—not just turn out a fine graphic piece.

My friend Joyce Kehoe makes writing possible for me. She turned my original composition into sharp computer form—yes, all twenty-two revisions. She helped with graphic decisions. Most importantly she was there to encourage.

I want to thank five special friends of fifty-plus years whose presence was a strong support during some long desert years: Dick and Betty Bohrer, Colette Poore, and John and Beverly West.

Without my prayer partners, this book would never have come to completion. I would especially like to acknowledge my indebtedness to five of them who prayed it through some of the critical times: Muriel Cook, Joyce, Colette, Corinne Repsold, and Linda Wright.

PART ONE

The Empty Desert

*Remember how the LORD your God led you
all the way in the desert these forty years,
to humble you and to test you in order to
know what was in your heart, whether or not
you would keep his commands.*

DEUTERONOMY 8:2

~ I ~

TREASURES IN THE SAND

"There they will offer righteous sacrifices;
For they will draw out the…
hidden treasures of the sand."

DEUTERONOMY 33:19, NASB

he trail emerged suddenly from the forest.

I stopped to catch my breath, looking out across a shimmering horizon that now seemed a million miles wide.

What was this? Where was I?

Sipping cool water from my canteen, I reflected on the trail just behind me. What a hike! I *lived* for such journeys! For mile after mile, my path had wound alongside a strong, young river that roared and leaped between deep pools, thundering over countless falls. Underfoot the trail had been soft, springy. On either side, filtered sunlight caressed ferns, moss-covered boulders, and lush undergrowth—a kaleidoscope of a thousand greens.

But now, more abruptly than I could have imagined, the forest was behind me.

My trail led away from the trees into a vast desert basin.

The river, my raucous companion for uncounted miles, had turned on itself and rushed back into its forest sanctuary. An unaccustomed silence lay heavy on my ears.

I stepped out with a quickened pace, eager now for the night's campground. Surely a dip in an alpine lake, a campfire, and a good night's sleep under the stars would set all mysteries to rights.

Yet even as I walked, doubts began to edge into my thoughts. *What was happening to my trail?* Turf gave way to unyielding gravel. The coolness of the forest ebbed under a relentless sun. Dust clung to my shoes. Then—to my dismay— the path itself began to fade, losing itself in scattered rock and trackless sand.

Where from here? Which way?

There were no signs, no markers, no footprints to follow. Nothing on the horizon in any direction but an oppressive emptiness, a great silent void. And I, who study maps so carefully and love to chart each mile of my trek, had not seen any desert at all on them.

Have you found yourself in such a place along life's winding ways? Has your path ever led you into a sun-scorched desert where you expected none? Are you there now? Standing perplexed in an uncharted wilderness? Asking yourself, "How did I walk into such a place?"

If so, it may be that these few treasures I have plucked from the sands of my desert journeys may strengthen your heart as you pass through your own desolate places.

There truly are treasures in the sand…but they do not lie on the surface, nor are they easily won.

For most of us, life holds a few desert stretches along the way— some short, some long. For others, the dry lands stretch on and on for countless, stumbling miles. Some deserts are forced upon us; some come of our own making. The desert speaks of barrenness, helplessness, and aching loneliness. It is a place of changeless deadness as far as the eye can see. It is a place where you travel on and on with neither landmark nor destination— and often no sign of God.

There are many such deserts in life, places where the very things that gave life meaning and direction have disappeared under shifting, blowing sand. Any one of these situations can produce such desolate seasons:

A drastic change in family circumstances…

A deep relationship severed…

An unwanted role imposed…

A debilitating illness…

An awareness of fading abilities…

A move into a strange new culture…

A life plan shattered…

An unyielding spiritual drought…

A lingering dispute with one you had called "friend"…

A sad, hopeless mood that won't let go….

Many young mothers, widows, childless couples, singles, retirees, and those in empty marriages have tasted such desolation, finding themselves crossing a wide, wild land in the heat of day and the chill of night.

The Lord has deep purposes in all such experiences—never doubt it! Yet in those bewildering sands of the wilderness, the fact of His personal leading in our lives is often lost to us.

The desert is the place where we meet God. It is the place of personal transformation. "Moses…led the flock to the far side of the desert….There the angel of the LORD appeared to him" (Exodus 3:1–2). Yes, *there*.

The desert is a symbol of trial, of testing. The Lord Himself speaks of the desert as "the great and terrible wilderness, with its fiery serpents and scorpions and thirsty ground where there was no water." His purpose in allowing you to experience it, He says, is to "do good for you in the end" (Deuteronomy 8:15, 16, NASB).

The desert is the place where He woos us to Himself. "I

will lead her into the desert and speak tenderly to her" (Hosea 2:14). There He shows us His deep, personal love.

The Lord has brought me across three kinds of deserts in my life journey, each very different. Quite honestly, I would not have chosen any of them. Yet looking back on my encounters with the Lord in those places, I now value my days in the barren lands as the pinnacle experiences of my life.

19

What do you do when the promises of God seem like hollow words, empty as the desert winds?

~2~

PROVISION IN
THE WILDERNESS

Who has the wisdom to count the clouds?
Who can tip over the water jars of the heavens
when the dust becomes hard
and the clods of earth stick together?

JOB 38:37-38

It was the most satisfying and fulfilling role I had ever experienced. It was one of those rare, intoxicating times in life when you find yourself in a place you are precisely prepared to fulfill. Think of a jigsaw puzzle with one remaining piece slipping into the very place arranged for it. Right shape, right colors, right edges—a perfect match!

I was a high school principal, esteemed in my community, used of God in the lives of students whose friendship and respect had been the joy of my life. My cup was full and brimming over.

Suddenly—with very little warning—the scene changed.

For what I felt to be a necessary stand, my relationship with the school was abruptly, irrevocably severed. Overnight, I became a virtual outcast from that community. It happened so quickly! Life that had been so rich with laughter, excitement, warmth of friends, companionship in work, and joy of ministry suddenly ceased.

Just like that, the trail turned.

Just like that, the forest ended.

Just like that, I found myself in an alien place—a desert as bleak as I could ever have imagined.

It was as though I had been stripped of my identity. *Who was I now?* I was no one, going nowhere, with nothing meaningful to do. *How could it happen?* How could I possess such richness of purpose and surety of goals one moment and find myself so utterly at a loss in the next? I was alone in an empty desert—a harsh environment that would swallow me up for several long years.

What do you do when you hit those stretches? Where do you turn when a pleasant forest trail abruptly dumps you into a wasteland, and you can't go back? What do you do in days of dull ache, searing pain, or paralyzing confusion?

The first thing to do is to watch for God's provision. He has a great deal of experience caring for His children in the wilderness.

I was reminded of these truths when I visited friends living on the southern Arabian Peninsula—a desert encompassing over a million square miles. From their home in an oasis city, we made forays out into those immense, empty regions.

At times, we found ourselves in an old-movie world of black and gray. In other regions, the sands glistened in Technicolor golds, pinks, reds, oranges, and browns. Vegetation, where you could find it, was sparse.

Three scenes of God's surprising provision stand out from those days.

23

Bouncing along in a Land Cruiser over a stretch of rolling dunes, my friends and I suddenly bogged down in soft sand, and the Land Cruiser refused to budge. The temperature that day simmered at 115 degrees, but it seemed much hotter as the glare of the desert sun radiated from the sand. Not far from where we were stuck, I noticed the bleached, white bones of a camel. I remember thinking, *This place bleaches out life—even of camels, the strongest and most suited to it.*

We let most of the air out of the tires and in the furnace heat made many futile attempts to lurch the vehicle out of its pit. Then, just when I had begun to wonder about our survival, the Land Cruiser suddenly broke free in one fluid movement—exactly as if the hand of God had lifted us from that place and sent us on our way again.

～ᔕᙢᴖ～

Another scene comes to mind.

We were crossing a seemingly endless plateau of sand that looked like the ashes of some great inferno of the past. Suddenly we encountered a deep, narrow gorge slicing through the plateau directly in front of us. Looking down into the cleft, we saw ribbons of green stretched out along both sides of a glistening stream of water, which eventually disappeared into the sands. The stream had its genesis in rainwater running off the slopes of faraway mountains. "It's called a *wadi*," my friends told me.

Finding an accessible spot, we clambered down into the gorge. At the head of the canyon, we found the place where the stream gushed from a massive wall of broken rock. It formed a large, very deep pool, shaded on three sides by overhanging rocks. The water was clear enough to see a small red stone at the bottom.

In that moment, as never before, I understood the meaning of *oasis*. There beneath the scorching desert floor, we found pure, cool refreshment. Water to drink—all one could want—

and enough for a skin-tingling swim in a pristine, crystal pool. For those few moments, we forgot all about the desert above us.

In a third experience, our day began with a long drive across a portion of desert that seemed paved with shale. My friends were taking me to a vista that offered a superb view of the desert stretching beyond.

When we crested the top of the rise, my friends leaped from the vehicle, mute with wonder. Instead of the expected sea of sand, we looked down on mile after mile of undulating grasslands pasturing herds of camels and goats. Suddenly finding their voices, my companions shouted aloud, almost in unison:

"It has rained!"

Again and again they exclaimed to each other, "It has *RAINED!*" Never in all their years there had they seen the sight that was now before them.

Your personal desert—whatever it may be—may make you feel as if you have stalled in a pit where you can move neither forward nor backward. God will lift you out of that helpless place. He "led us through the wilderness," wrote the prophet, "through a land of deserts and pits" (Jeremiah 2:6, NKJV).

At unexpected times and in unlooked-for ways, He will be a cool, refreshing wadi to you. "Water will gush forth in the wilderness…. The burning sand will become a pool" (Isaiah 35:6-7).

His purpose is to transform your parched heart into lush, green grassland. He will lead you into green pastures, by still waters, where you *will* find refreshment and provision.

At times, He will lead you into a desert place to tell you of His tender love. "Who is this coming up from the wilderness, leaning upon her beloved?" (Song of Solomon 8:5, NKJV).

27

The God of heaven will "spread a table in the desert" (Psalm 78:19).

But what do you do—where do you turn—when these promises of God seem like hollow words, empty as the desert winds? How do you journey on when there are no provisions as far as your straining eyes can see? What happens to hope when life becomes a vast desert without beginning or end, without so much as a withered plant on the horizon?

No matter how wide your wilderness, God knows how to care for His own. He will teach you lesson by lesson how to cross the desert…and enter into a richer territory than you have ever known.

3

ALIEN LANDSCAPE

*I will instruct you and teach you
in the way you should go;
I will counsel you and watch over you.
Do not be like the horse or the mule,
which have no understanding
but must be controlled by bit and bridle
or they will not come to you.*

PSALM 32:8–9

The loss of my cherished position as a principal certainly brought me into a dry, alien land—a desert such as I have never experienced.

Stripped of my position, my identity, and a circle of dear friends, my first great challenge was to let go of the past. I knew that I must—or sink into a bitterness or despair from which I might never emerge.

Yet I couldn't seem to release my grip.

"LET GO"

All of the scenes, all of the voices, seemed to play over and over again in my mind. *What if I had done this? What if I had said that? What if I had proved point A? What if I had yielded on point B? Was it my fault after all? Did I sin in this?*

Surely this was just a short detour, I assured myself. A temporary setback. Certainly I could find a position (after eight years of experience!) just like the one I'd left. Maybe better!

I looked.

For a long time I searched high and low for that similar position. I chased leads, followed up on contacts, knocked on doors. But there was nothing. My phone never rang. My mailbox stayed empty. At one point, I pursued a cherished dream and tried to start a Christian high school myself. When at the last heartbreaking minute that plan fell through, it became clear to me that this way of life was over. Forever.

God was saying, "My daughter, it's time to let go."

Let go? What a frightening, desolate prospect! It tasted like death. *Let go?* That meant crossing the nightmare heart of the desert—straight through the heat and deadness and pain—rather than skirting its edges.

Yes, I had always believed (in a theoretical sense) that "God was my all-in-all." I believed He was who He claimed to be. But now I was forced to step out in naked faith and *prove* His sufficiency in my life.

I would have to put the past pleasures and satisfactions right out of my mind and endure the ache of barrenness. I would have to put to death those dreams of "what might have been" or "what might be."

Difficult as this letting go may have been mentally, letting go emotionally was sheer agony. The emotional yearning to have the old satisfactions back again kept the wound perpetually open. Each refusal to let myself indulge those longings—each slamming of that door—hurt me to the marrow of my bones.

Letting go took a long time.

I couldn't hurry it. It was a season of grief that I had to walk through one step at a time.

31

"FORGIVE"

I had denied any anger over the past events by glossing over them. ("I'm a good Christian! Good Christians don't get angry, do they?")

But all the while…I sensed it was there. It was like a brackish desert well, seeping up from the depths, with water so bitter that even thirsty camels would refuse to drink. My anger was real, and it kept me emotionally attached to a dead past.

I had to face it.

I had to forgive those who had wounded me, rejected me, turned away from me. I had to love my enemy. What was the alternative? Hate? Bitterness? Vengeance? Terminal cynicism?

The Lord led me gently down a path I did not want to

walk—but *had* to walk if I was to follow Him. And I did walk that way, though I could neither rush nor run.

During that season of great struggle, I became acutely aware that *I could not do any of these things alone.* Without help, I would never get out of that desert. My strength was bleached out like those long-remembered camel bones. In the midst of my appalling weakness, I was surprised to find the Spirit's presence there with me, enabling me to let go, finger by clenched finger. Enabling me to forgive, word by word, deed by deed. And the greatest miracle—enabling me to love. In a word, He lifted me out of the pit in which I was stuck.

It also took time to lay down my anger at the situation in which I found myself. I did not *want* this kind of life. Not at all!

Through much struggle, God brought me to the place where, from deep within, I chose to accept the reality of my situation and its pain. (It was an exercise I had to repeat again and again.)

Acceptance won the day. What resignation, trying to forget, or distracting myself with a thousand activities could not accomplish, acceptance did. As Amy Carmichael wrote, "In acceptance lieth peace."

Perhaps, like me, you want to press on to the future without dealing with the past. The God of time and eternity knows that that won't work. The past that you have locked in a closet will begin rattling the door and will not remain silent. God wants His sons and daughters to walk in joy and true freedom. His lessons are hard, but His outcomes bring sweet release…and banish lingering shadows.

Therefore if the Son makes you free, you shall be free indeed.

JOHN 8:36, NKJV

God was saying, "My daughter, it's time to let go."

4

SILENT WAITING

Who is among you that fears the LORD,
That obeys the voice of His servant,
That walks in darkness and has no light?
Let him trust in the name of
the LORD and rely on his God.

ISAIAH 50:10, NASB

*E*ncouraged by His help, I began to imagine I had turned a corner—that the worst part of the desert journey was over.

I was wrong. A hurdle loomed before me that seemed even more impossible than letting go and laying down my anger.

Now my task was to "let rest."

"LET REST"

During the long process of letting go, I'd at least had something to occupy my energies.

Now there was nothing to do.

Yes, I had left the past behind, but…what was ahead?

Where was my destination?

Where were the milestones?

I, the goal-oriented climber of summits, had nothing to conquer. The desert was a flat, featureless plain—an infinity of space where the sands merged into the sky. I had no vision, no driving purpose. Oh yes, I had a job that paid the rent, some Bible classes to teach, and a start on some new friendships—*but something was missing.*

I still had no focus. No bull's-eye in my target—in fact, no target at all. I felt utterly confused, disconnected, and bored in this monotonous desert. Did my life have any meaning? *Eternal* meaning? Questions haunted me in the night: *Who am I? Why am I? Where am I going?* At His bidding I had put aside everything I held dear for the sake of ministry—plans for marriage, my architectural profession. And now there was no ministry. I needed a ministry to have a life that felt complete.

It seemed wrong to be so…unproductive. Surely life was more than occupying space on the planet. More than feeding and clothing myself. More than the monotonic round of day after day. Where were the inner fires? My whole identity had been so tied to accomplishing that I couldn't bear giving my life to nothingness. I used to have a grip on the steering wheel, but now everything seemed completely out of my hands.

I had come at last to the great lesson of the empty desert—

the stark reality that *I am not the one in ultimate control*. For the first time I realized how deeply committed I had been to being in charge of my life—of being able to avoid dissatisfying situations and to make a satisfying life for myself in the midst of difficult ones. Now I found myself utterly dependent on God to give meaning to my life. There was nothing to do but wait on Him. I felt as alone and helpless as I had ever felt in my life.

How long, *how long* would this go on? Why this waste of the best years of my life? When would rain wash across my dry landscape, bringing the green? And where was God in all of this? Why was He so silent? Had He forgotten me? Had He? Where were the opportunities to serve His kingdom? Where was that magnificent sense of significance? Was this all there was to life? Why didn't He speak?

How hard it was to let things rest. Everything in me wanted to search and scour the landscape, grasping at whatever straws of significance came within reach. Several times I pursued such avenues of self-sustained fulfillment—only to find myself as hollow and destitute of spirit as ever.

So there I was—totally dependent on a silent God to sustain me. When the desolation within me seemed wider than the Sahara, I had to wait on Him to fill the empty places.

It seemed so unfair. So painful.

The temptation to despair was strong. Why even desire purpose or meaning? Why hope? Why set myself up for my disappointment? "God has nothing for you," the Tempter hissed. "You have failed Him. He is through with you." It took faith and repeated acts of the will to say, "I *will* hope in God. I *will* believe that He has a purpose and plan for my life. I *will* believe that He has a reason for this silence, that He is working something deep within me. I *will* believe He is holding me in His hands."

It was the memory of His past goodnesses, large and small, that gave the energy for that choice.

The psalmist wrote:

38

> *My soul, wait in silence for God only,*
> *For my hope is from Him.*

PSALM 62:5, NASB

It would have seemed easier in that moment to scale the almost sheer side of one of the seven hundred-foot-high dunes of the Arabian Desert than to wait in absolute trust on God.

But what could I do? I found myself just where Peter had stood millennia before, when he said to Jesus, "Master, to whom shall we go? You alone have the words that give eternal life" (John 6:68, TLB). God alone had the answers to my questions, too. I knew that. Ultimate purpose and meaning lay with Him and nowhere else. I would simply have to wait for Him to open His path.

Wait!

By nature I am angry at having to wait for much of anything. Waiting stops me in my tracks of getting what I want. Now I was being called on to experience my dependence and to wait for One I couldn't control. I was being asked to trust Him at a much deeper level—to believe He had a reason for this barren season of my life. Only the God of hope can give us the patience, endurance, and faith to wait humbly in silence before Him.

You will find, as I found then and have found so many times since, that He is able.

Only the God of hope can give us the patience, endurance, and faith to wait humbly in silence before Him.

~5~

A CHANGE OF PERSPECTIVE

But whatever things were gain to me,
those things I have counted
as loss for the sake of Christ.

PHILIPPIANS 3:7 NASB

*I*t wasn't only the emptiness of my days that distressed me; I felt as though *I* was being emptied out. All the old, mostly false images I had cherished of myself were being peeled away, layer by layer. I began to understand how I had used my productivity and accomplishments to validate my being.

I had always told myself that I staked my personal value on the fact of my relationship to the Lord. I knew all about the glorious identity I had in Him. I had studied it. Diagrammed it. Taught it. I knew myself to be "the beloved child of the Father, the bride of Christ, the vessel of the Spirit." I knew all that— mentally. Now I realized that deep down I had been out to show myself and others that I had value because I had something to offer. Yes, I had always *said* that He was sufficient for my heart's deepest needs; but now I realized I wanted something more.

Pride, self-sufficiency, complacency, independence, self-righteousness—how much ungodliness began to show itself in the pitiless light of His desert sun. So much for which to repent! The Lord who opened the eyes of the blind began to reveal my own blind spots, so I could see more deeply who I was by nature and mourn over it. At last I realized there was no good thing in me apart from Him.

At this place where I met myself, seeing myself as I truly was, I met God.

I saw Him with outstretched arms.

I felt encircled in His love.

In the face of my sinfulness, He was cherishing me. Nothing, nothing in the universe could compare with being so unconditionally loved. To be the object of His love and to respond to it was what made life meaningful. *He* was the purpose and the goal of life. He held me in His strong hands and was working out *His* eternal purposes through me. He was the "good land—a land with streams and pools of water, with springs flowing in the valleys and hills" (Deuteronomy 8:7).

He reminded me of the magnificent truth about myself that the desert sands had covered. It was a truth I had known as a fact but little as a reality. It hadn't seemed all that important to me. Now it came into my view as the very stream of life.

Here is the essence of that truth: Sin may intrude in my life, but at the core of my being, I am a new creation. When I received the Lord, He implanted new life—His life—into the lifeless desert of my heart. He said to me, "Lift up your head. Walk in the dignity and splendor of the new creation that you are—the real you. I am within you to bring forth My right responses as each occasion arises. Depend on Me for this. Furthermore, rivers of water— streams in the desert—will flow from you. Yes, from you."

The grid through which I saw things also shifted. *He* was my life. Not my ministry. Not my dreams of happiness. Only the long season in the empty desert could have accomplished such a total deep inward change. The vacant, burning sands were now full of His presence—and more to be desired than a world of rich, cool forests.

43

Laying down my ceaseless striving, I was content to accept my limitations—to embrace them as the very things that kept me dependent upon God.

I found God in the common, ordinary, everyday things of life. I saw that it was in the rough and tumble of that life, with its peaks and deep valleys, that the life of Christ was formed in me and expressed itself through me, and that that alone is ministry.

The desert had done a transforming work in me. It had

given me new eyes and a new freedom from old compulsions and preoccupations. My spirit reveled in the delightful sense of His immediacy—His nearness to every waking thought.

And I worshiped Him.

44

THE DESERT WITHIN THE DESERT

*They roamed the parched land
in desolate wastelands at night.*

JOB 30:3

The Arabs call it the "Empty Quarter."

In the great Arabian Desert, there is a vast terrain so forsaken, so unforgivably hostile to life, that it is known as "the desert within the desert." The Empty Quarter has long been regarded one of the harshest slices of real estate on earth.

Spiritually, this nightmare landscape symbolizes what many through the ages have called "the dark night of the soul." In one unforgettable season of my life, God led me to that place and then…it was as though He walked away.

Out of nowhere, without explanation, my heart became dead toward the Lord. Once-loved music failed to stir me.

Devotional times felt as dry and useless as counting pebbles on a planet of stones. There was no sense of the Lord's presence. No desire to reach out to Him. Prayer was like trying to slog through knee-deep sand. It was dull, boring, tedious work, with none of the former warmth or fervency. Scriptures that had spoken to me for years with such urgency and tenderness went dead flat. I might as well have been reading the phone book.

Contemplating the Lord's glorious qualities did not touch my heart. Picturing Him in some familiar gospel scene failed to pierce my malaise.

48

If God had been on the other end of some cosmic phone line, the connection had either gone dead, or He had simply left the receiver off the hook and taken Himself elsewhere.

That was not what I wanted!

That was not what I needed!

Didn't He realize that? Didn't the One who made me and formed me know the kind of emotional connection I needed with Him? I wanted some emotional returns from my relationship with God. Was that so unreasonable? I wanted a love I could feel, a love that would enable me to respond in kind.

A DECLARATION OF DEPENDENCE

For years, I had always said that I wanted God for Himself alone. It was clear now that I wanted the relationship for what it could do for ME.

My spiritual self-confidence, my spiritual achievement, and, in fact, my spirituality were gone. I was left with nothing.

How I craved the satisfaction of offering something lovely and significant to God. But He had dropped me in the Empty Quarter, the desert within the desert, and I had nothing to offer Him or others. I was hollow.

What was I to DO? Simply accept the emptiness? Wait in the Empty Quarter until—sometime, somehow—He came to me again?

What would it mean if I stopped seeking after feelings? What would it mean to simply rely on His Word—His promises alone—even if I could never again experience the feelings I had savored in days gone by? WHAT WOULD IT MEAN?

It would mean letting go of the "truth" of my feelings and accepting His truth—that He loves me infinitely and unconditionally.

It would mean setting His promises above my feelings.

It would mean believing that He was working out His purposes through me.

It would mean resting in the hands of God, whom I could not feel or detect.

It would mean resigning my will to His and letting Him water my desert how, when, and if He would.

After all was said and done, it was His business to transform my desert heart; my business was to simply invite Him into my emptiness. The earth itself was once "formless and empty, darkness was over the surface of the deep." Yet out of that black void God called forth light, life, and beauty and declared it good.

I would have to wait on the Creator God to do His work in me. Giving Him control of my spiritual life in that way was one of the most difficult surrenders I had ever made. It was signing my declaration of dependence. It was signing a death warrant to so much that I had cherished, including the thought that I could make myself more spiritual. Sadly, I realized that many such attempts had been nothing more than spiritual ego trips. There are no do-it-yourself kits in the spiritual life.

Now was the time to rest in hope. Now was the time to believe that He was doing His work in and through me.

In the meantime, my emotions were barren—like the skeletons of trees half buried in the drifting sands. But what did that matter? What did it matter if I never felt *anything* again? Faith said that it was time to declare my love for Him—to set myself to please Him in all things, without demanding any mental or emotional return.

Through it all, feelings or not, it meant maintaining my expressions of love: diligently reading what He says about Himself in His Word, obeying His words, opening my heart to Him in prayer.

It was a time to present myself day by day at His feet, submitting to His will for my life for the next twenty-four hours.

It was a time to welcome my neediness as an opportunity to renew my dependence.

It was a time to begin acting in love to people, moment by moment, regardless of feelings toward them or response from them.

It was a time to just accept God's silence, in the belief that the Holy Spirit was at work in me on some deeper level beyond my puny discernment.

It was a time to learn to be silent before Him.

Slowly I found myself resting in God alone: in His sufficiency for my utter weakness, in the gift of His righteousness for my sinfulness, and, above all, in His declaration of unconditional love. Sometimes I had small tastes of that love—emotionally and mentally. If ever there were a cool wadi for my heart, this was it. I was the little red rock at the bottom of the great pool, totally submerged in my Father's love. For a few brief, exhilarating moments, I could forget the desert. Then I would be back into it again…keeping my eyes on the blank horizon…hoping for a more continuously realized fellowship with Him. But not demanding it!

A strange joy came as I began to see Him work through me, even when I had no sense of His presence. Was this to be the new pattern of life? One thing I knew, whether or whenever He chose to give or withhold any sense of it, I now had a deep confidence in His loving presence and a clearer picture of the walk of faith.

Then one day…it happened.

He "tipped over the water jars of the heavens," flooding me with a sense of His love far deeper than I had ever experienced or imagined. Again He "turned my mourning into dancing." Truly. The joy was beyond description.

For so long I had been asking, as Moses did at the burning bush, "Who am I?" My question now changed to Moses' next question, "Lord, *who are You?*"

God's answer was, "I AM."

Who is the I AM—the self-existent One? He is the Creator, the Life giver. He is the God of good eternal purposes who unfailingly carries them out. He had done deep things in me in that silent wasteland, preparing me for His next purpose—His last lesson in the empty desert.

"LET ME"

And what was that purpose?

He wanted some of His children fed!

His word to me was not "Pam, My daughter, I want to give you meaning in life." He Himself was now that. It was instead, "There are sheep of Mine that need feeding. I want you to be grassland for them to pasture on. Let Me make you that—

52

a source of life in this scene of death. Remember, you are an emptiness to be continuously filled with Me. You 'are *not.*' I AM."

For some people, His purpose is a very deep but hidden ministry, oftentimes hidden from their own eyes. Their lives continue outwardly humdrum, ordinary. But from them, God pours life-giving water on others.

A woman named Biddie Chambers comes to mind.

Most of us have heard of *My Utmost for His Highest,* by Oswald Chambers. It is read worldwide, refreshing millions upon millions, and considered by many the most influential devotional book of all time.

Chambers's wife, Biddie, widowed at thirty-three, compiled this devotional from her meticulous notes of his sermons and then personally published it (and fifty subsequent titles!). She lived in poverty and obscurity through many years of her fifty-year widowhood. But what torrents of life have cascaded through her painstaking work!

Yes, from the empty, dependent one, streams of living water will always flow. We are a vessel of the Holy Spirit.

In my own life, God opened up a broad ministry after my sojourn in the empty desert. This was the kingdom work He had in mind for me before the foundation of the world. This was the work the empty desert had prepared me for. I was now with college students; teaching, counseling, training men and women—intimately involved in the lives of many at a much deeper level than ever before. Opportunities abounded to impact women in seminars and conferences. And yes, the door opened for a writing ministry beyond what I had ever conceived.

Yet all of these things were not to be "my life," but rather the overflow of His. I could truly sing, "All my springs of joy are in you" (Psalm 87:7, NASB). The rain of His grace had transformed my sea of sand into grasslands. I could shout, "It has rained!"

"For the pastures of the wilderness have turned green" (Joel 2:22, NASB).

54

O Living Stream; O gracious rain,
None wait for Thee, and wait in vain.

—TER STEEGEN

In the empty desert,
the Spirit transforms.

PART TWO

The Testing Desert

Their tongue is parched with thirst;
I, the LORD, will answer them Myself.

ISAIAH 41:17, NASB

~7~

ACROSS THE MOJAVE

He led you through the vast and dreadful desert,
that thirsty and waterless land,
with its venomous snakes and scorpions.

DEUTERONOMY 8:15

*D*eserts of the heart leave us vulnerable.

Have you found this to be true? Vulnerable in the areas we least expect....

In the summer following World War II, my mother and I drove across the country. I was taking on a new position "out West," and my old car (sans air conditioning) was laden with as many household possessions as we could wedge inside. Tires for civilian use had not yet come on the market; my four were heavily patched and bulging ominously on the sidewalls.

At the proverbial Last Chance Gas Station before crossing the Mojave Desert, the attendant repeated what a number of

men had already told us: "You two women shouldn't be travel-
ing alone on tires like those! 'Specially across this desert. Drive
very slowly—and only on cool pavement. Travel at night and
take plenty of water—as much as you can carry—for the
desert."

I nodded politely, thanking him for his concern. Inside,
however, I didn't take it seriously. The man was obviously
exaggerating. He probably assumed we were helpless East Coast
females who would faint at the first sign of trouble. A lot he
knew! Hadn't we just traversed three thousand miles? Hadn't
I repaired several blowouts with my own two hands? Hadn't I
survived New York City heat and humidity for years on end?

Had the station attendant mentioned fiery serpents, I
would have calmly assured him that as an experienced hiker
I knew perfectly well how to deal with snakebites. And I was
smugly certain I could handle this western desert with the
funny name.

I filled our two thermoses and an old army canteen with
water. ("That should certainly be enough!") Shooting up a
quick prayer for the Lord's protection, we started out at five that
August morning.

It was pleasantly cool. Eventually we arrived at the desert.
It was mostly pebbly and dull gray, dotted with sage and cacti.
A monotonous place. Flat for long stretches, the highway occa-
sionally dropped to a lower plain, then made a long, slow climb

back up onto the plateau on the other side.

The sun crested the eastern horizon by six.

By nine, it was warm.

By ten, it was hot.

By eleven, it was *blazing*.

Remembering the station attendant's counsel, I had slowed down to twenty-five miles per hour—just before the unexpected happened.

THE UNEXPECTED

On a long rise the radiator suddenly boiled over, enveloping us in an angry cloud of steam. There was nothing to do but stop, wait patiently in the baking heat until the engine cooled, pour in some water, and go on. Somewhat shaken, I slowed our pace to twenty miles per hour.

On another rise, however, it happened again. And again. And again. What could I do? There were no cell phones in those days, and I was helpless to fix this problem. In the days immediately following the war, people didn't travel across this desert as much as they would just a few years later. In that entire long journey across the desert, I don't remember seeing another car.

We had to save all of our water for the radiator, and I was already thirsty. Have you ever suffered from thirst? I don't mean the casual, almost thoughtless impulse that prompts you to drift to the water fountain for a sip or two. I mean *urgent* thirst. Not only was I thirsty, but my overheated engine was desperately in need of water. The radiator kept boiling over, and by noon we had no water left to pour in. Not a drop.

Thoroughly frightened now, my cocksureness burned away in the overwhelming heat. New York City had never felt like this! As the miles crept by, I implored the Lord for help. Sometimes, in the hottest part of that endless afternoon, a little cloud drifted by overhead, giving us a bit of cooling—not to mention relief for the overheated engine and threadbare tires. I saw those clouds as the Lord's very personal care for me in the face of my foolish self-confidence.

Would we be able to make it?

Would the engine melt down and leave us stranded in this desert?

Anxiety grew exponentially as we crawled across this interminable stretch of hades. Then, after some of the longest hours of my life, we saw something on the shimmering horizon. A dot. A smudge. No…a town! *And water!* The Lord had personally taken me across the blazing Mojave. I would never again take its threats lightly. After that experience, I never wanted to cross a desert again—or even see one, if I could help it.

Just a few years later, however, I relented—and the Lord arranged a journey through a corner of the Mojave in springtime. Though I had read of it and seen pictures of it, I could not believe my eyes.

The drab, tedious desert had been transformed into a wonderland of exploding color and beauty as far as my eyes could see in every direction. Timely rain and warmth had kissed the dry lands into magnificent full bloom.

Sitting on a twig near where I stood, a little bird—one tiny additional daub of color in that joyous landscape—sang his lungs out.

The Lord was saying, "When I take you through a blazing desert full of fiery serpents, this is the end I have in sight for you."

To this very day, the fragrance of that springtime in the desert lives in my memory.

One thing I have learned:
The Promiser keeps
His promises.

8

The Serpent Bites

For we do not have a high priest
who is unable to sympathize with our weaknesses,
but we have one who has been tempted in every way,
just as we are—yet was without sin.
Let us then approach the throne of grace with
confidence, so that we may receive mercy and find
grace to help us in our time of need.

Hebrews 4:15–16

In one of life's searing desert expanses, I met a temptation. And the fiery serpent bit.

Somehow, I never thought I'd have to deal with this particular temptation. Yet if by chance I ever should meet it, I had told myself, I was certain I could handle it. After all, I'd managed it quite efficiently for years.

Early in my twenties, I answered the Lord's call to celibacy. He was calling me to devote myself completely to His interests through the days of my life. From that time on, I trusted Him to meet my needs for provision, protection, and emotional satisfaction.

And He did. The single-minded focus gave me many expanded opportunities to serve Him.

Then, some years later, deep longings broke through the walls of what I had always considered a secure, steel box. I had personally placed those desires in that box, firmly closed the lid, and locked it with a padlock.

What was happening to me? Why were those feelings acting up NOW? I tried to stuff the errant emotions back into that firm control structure I had always maintained. Much to my dismay—I couldn't! My strength evaporated in the face of suddenly overpowering demands. Trying to distract myself or pretending the pain wasn't there no longer made the ache subside. Throwing myself into work, which had always been my surefire method of quieting occasional muffled rumblings, failed completely. My interior engine was approaching meltdown.

As an adolescent, an occasional fantasy had served from time to time as an emotional pacifier. But now it was like gasoline on a bonfire. My heart was thirsty. Desperately thirsty. I found myself overcome with longing for that which every woman longs—to be pursued, held, highly valued, found delightful, and tenderly cherished. I ached for sexual fulfillment and children to love and nourish.

What was happening to me?

Where was God—whom I'd always trusted to satisfy my longings? I was doing everything I knew to develop a deeper intimacy with Him. But that wasn't stopping the pangs. I was thirsty as could be, and there was no water. The serpent coiled in the sand told me (as he had Eve) that the things I was missing should be mine.

Fantasy became temptation's fiery bite.

I knew it was wrong. It was saying, "Lord, You're not satisfying my needs the way I want. I'll get them met myself." Regardless, I gave my imagination full rein, creating idols and images as it would. I told myself dozens of times that the fantasizing must stop. It was going further—much further—than I'd planned.

I'd always had a strong will and had been trained from childhood to discipline my mind and emotions. Yet despite all resolves, when the pressure came, I would cave in. Time after time. Redoubling my efforts, crying out to the Lord for strength, just didn't work. With my self-confidence in tatters, I struggled on without much hope.

One bleak day, looking into that serpent's cold, lidless eyes, it became clear to me that my will—even with the Lord's help—would never be enough. I realized that I was utterly powerless and that the only

71

answer was to admit the fact and cling to the Lord for sheer mercy and grace.

I was also angry—angry with myself for not being able to overcome temptation.

Why didn't He simply strengthen my will? Why didn't He enable me, instead of expecting me to come crawling to Him to admit my weakness and powerlessness and to beg for mercy and grace?

Grace, amazing as it might be, was not a "sweet sound" to my pride that day. The sheer intensity of my anger shocked and appalled me. In brokenness, I pleaded for forgiveness. Humbly turning to Jesus as my living High Priest, I asked Him for "mercy and grace to help" in my time of need.

Then the rains came, gentle and sweet.

The rain of grace fell on the parched soil of my heart. I found the Lord Jesus to be the merciful High Priest He said He was. He reminded me (how could I have forgotten?) that He knew what it meant to "suffer, being tempted." Jesus had been tempted in *every way*, just as I was. He had endured the suffering—not ended it by yielding.

Gently, He encouraged me to do the same, assuring me He could enable me to stand.

How I loved Him! As the Scripture says, "She who has been forgiven much, loves much."

72

Then the rains came,
gentle and sweet.

9

FLOWERS IN THE DESERT

*Because he himself suffered when he was
tempted, he is able to help those
who are being tempted.*

HEBREWS 2:18

*D*eliverances often came in the midst of my daily struggles with temptation.

Little clouds brought relief in the heat of battle.

It was a comfort knowing that the Lord Jesus was able to feel my pain, to sympathize with my weakness. His eyes, ever on me, were filled with love and compassion, not disgust. Besides all of that, He was earnestly praying for me before the Father's throne. I realized that condemning myself and using the whip of guilt were no match for the power of temptation. Only my Lord's indwelling presence could conquer. I learned to rely on that alone.

I had never been closer to the Lord. I clung to Him in deep dependence, fearing to let go even for a moment. As we walked together through this desert, He showed me ways to escape temptation's enticement. He taught me to flee at the first second of mental imaging, not five seconds later at the point of no return. He was there to comfort. He was there to strengthen and help me tolerate the emptiness left by the withdrawal of satisfaction.

With Him beside me, I knew I could endure my thirst and that eventually there would be water—a city of hope on the desert horizon. His tender love during those days drew my heart into an ever-deepening love for Him. It was that love that moved me, by the Spirit's power, to finally turn from the idols of my imagination.

The God of all grace Himself had restored me. I was the little bird on the twig singing my lungs out. The warmth of His love and the rain of grace and truth had done their good work in me.

Though I had mentally assented to it, I had never faced the utter corruption of my heart. I knew there were bad spots—areas as corrupt as could be. But, unknowingly, I held on to the idea that part was good, too. After all, there were things I would never do, words I would never say. In my prayers, I confessed the bad but held tightly onto my "good" and didn't want to let it go. The blazing desert had shown me my sinful, self-righteous heart—and the enormity of His grace. With my image of myself now shattered, I found that my only goodness was the gift of Christ's perfect righteousness.

As the days went by, that wondrous gift (deposited in my personal account) became so much more than a doctrine to me. It was a daily reality in which I reveled. Yes, I still fell on occasion. I still returned to the old idols in moments of empty weakness. But I hurried to confess those sins, knowing that I would receive forgiveness and then enjoy full fellowship standing before the Father's throne—*cleansed and faultless*—dressed in the dazzling white robe of Christ's righteousness, overwhelmed with joy and a gratitude beyond my power to describe, celebrating His infinite love.

He reminded me that at the center of my being I was not Gomer, the one who went to other lovers, but the new person, Hephzibah, "My delight is in her." Hephzibah was "a crown of beauty…a royal diadem" in the hand of God, that as a bridegroom rejoices over the bride, so God rejoiced over her. (See Isaiah 62:3–5.) He wanted me to see His view of me, His joy and delight in me, and above all to enjoy His love.

TWO FLOWERS

Two flowers of Christ's nature in me came into bloom as a result of the serpent's bite. One was a deep compassion for others struggling with any kind of temptation. I knew the bleak reality that with the right pressure, apart from God's grace, I would be where any of them were. My heart has been with fellow strugglers from that time on.

The other flower was humility. Following those days, I didn't have to try to be humble or pray for humility. I had seen something of my own heart, and that was enough to humble anyone! I knew all too well that only His grace could keep that flower from withering in the hot winds of pride. "Lead me not into temptation but deliver me from evil," became (and remains) my daily heart cry.

Yet more breathtakingly beautiful than a worldwide carpet of wildflowers was the One who had captivated my heart. Through the Bible, I knew Him as "the great High Priest." Through trial and temptation, I came to know Him at a deep, personal level as *my* High Priest who loved me intensely. He was loving enough to use His sword to strip away my false image of myself and expose the corruption of my heart. In the face of my anger, He persisted in love. He intimately knew my sinfulness, and His love for me was unchanged.

Unconditional love was a reality now. What security! What rest! He was strong enough to uphold me under the temptations and give me the grace that enabled me to stand. His compassion and tender care touched the deepest places of my heart. His love was more satisfying than anything on earth could ever be. I knew that under all my desire, it was His perfect love for which I had really been longing. I knew with that deep inward knowing that I was highly valued, found delightful, and tenderly cherished by Him.

Yes, I was passing through a land of thirsty ground and fiery serpents. Yes, there was a desert in my heart that left me vulnerable.

Yet His purpose was "to do me good in the end"—to water that desert and show me the power of His indwelling presence.

And He has.

*In the testing desert,
the High Priest supports.*

e day or night,

circumstances,

ntensely loved.

PART THREE

Springs in the Desert

Then will the eyes of the blind be opened....
The burning sand will become a pool,
the thirsty ground bubbling springs.

ISAIAH 35:5, 7

10

OASIS

He changes a wilderness into a pool of water
And a dry land into springs of water.

PSALM 107:35, NASB

he highway was a thin gray ribbon stretched across the empty miles.

I was driving up from Southern California through a desolate land of sagebrush, tumbleweed, and cacti. As the arrow-straight road began a long descent, I found myself glad for the change. *Any* change.

But when I caught my first glimpse of the country into which I descended, my heart fell like a stone.

This was Death Valley.

And it looked like it.

What in the name of sweet sanity had possessed me to travel to such a place? THIS was where I was to spend my long-anticipated vacation? THIS was where I had come for refreshment?

The travel agent, I concluded, must also deal in used bridges in Brooklyn. As far as my eye could see, this was the most barren, ugly place imaginable. It seemed nothing more than a vast plain, stretching to the horizon, littered with dark rubble, broken only by occasional salt flats. One spot I passed almost made me laugh out loud. It was a shallow pool of water with a sign posted at its edge: "Badwater." The fine print informed the traveler that the immediate area was home for a rare, infinitesimal snail and pickleweed.

Snails and pickleweed! Yes, indeed, I chided myself, *you certainly know how to pick a vacation paradise.* I later found out that the area was also home to "Devil's Golf Course"—not your traditional eighteen holes, but an expanse of jagged, three-foot-high pinnacles of crusted salt.

Death Valley's severe desolation reminded me of scenes sent back from the robot explorer on Mars.

Why, oh why, had I chosen to come HERE? I could have explored mountain trails! I could have walked along the crashing surf!

Then I rounded a curve in the road—and my view dramatically changed. What a transformation! Suddenly I found myself looking across a long stretch of green so intense it almost seemed to glow. Densely packed trees—date palms, tamarisks, mesquite—loomed out of a landscape that only a few miles back could barely sustain a few withered strands of desert grass.

What was this? How had I rounded one bend in the road and traveled from Mars to Eden?

Later, as I walked along the path to my little cabin among the graceful palms, the answer became apparent. Alongside all of the trees were small troughs brimming with clear, softly flowing water. It was the water that made life not only possible, but luxuriant in that arid waste.

89

Water? In this searing desert? Where had it come from? Surely they wouldn't pipe it all the way from the Sierras!

It came, I learned, from two great springs—two wondrous, God-made artesian wells, continuously gushing water from deep in the earth. Today, through a network of underground pipes, those springs produce enough sweet, cold water to meet the needs of a million visitors a year.

I was stunned to learn that Death Valley itself sits atop a mighty aquifer. Down, down below the desert floor, lie ten to twenty thousand feet of soil *saturated* with water. This vast underground reservoir constantly moves downward through myriad channels, over and under plates of rock. When it hits a vertical plane of rock, it gurgles to the surface as a spring of ever-flowing water.

Death Valley is said to be the hottest place on earth. Furnace Creek Wash, bisecting its length, deserves its name! Some months the temperature climbs to 120 degrees daily and has been recorded as high as 134. Desert windstorms shriek across the valley, propelling dust one hundred feet in the air and whipping sand and gravel like buckshot.

Here are miles and miles of lifeless wilderness, and in the midst of it all, a glorious green oasis, watered by two springs from the great underground aquifer.

I went to see those springs. They were far off the beaten track and hard to find. But suddenly, in the middle of the plain, I saw a ribbon of azure blue so intense that I couldn't believe it was water. *All heaven must be reflected in that water,* I said to myself. Following this stream, I came upon one of the springs. It was a deep, morning-glory blue pool edged by dark brown grasses. The quiet waters were breathtakingly beautiful in this monotonous landscape. So *this* was the source of the oasis!

90

Back at the resort, seated in a lawn chair beneath the wide fronds of a date palm, I closed my eyes to listen to the soft trickle of flowing water. In that moment, I couldn't help but consider what I needed so desperately in my own life.

How can I keep alive to You, Lord, when I'm being whipped by life's desert winds, sand blowing in my eyes, and the sun darkened by dust clouds? What can keep me when the long, straight desert highway stretches before me for as far as my weary eyes can see? What hope do I have in my heart as I live out my life in a world that I cannot change—a world full of poverty, injustice, starvation, cruelty, killings, sadness, and death? How can I keep green and growing in the midst of disappointments, discouragements, and disillusionments—through the ugly stretches when I am misunderstood, maligned, devalued? Is there any way back to Eden?

"No," He seemed to say to me, "that way is closed to you and barred. But listen—I have a place far, far better. I am the way there. Let Me remind you of one of the great springs that produces the oasis in this Death Valley of life. I showed you this spring at the beginning of your walk with Me. Remember? You have let the sands drift in, My daughter, blocking the flow. Dig it out and drink—drink deeply—once again."

91

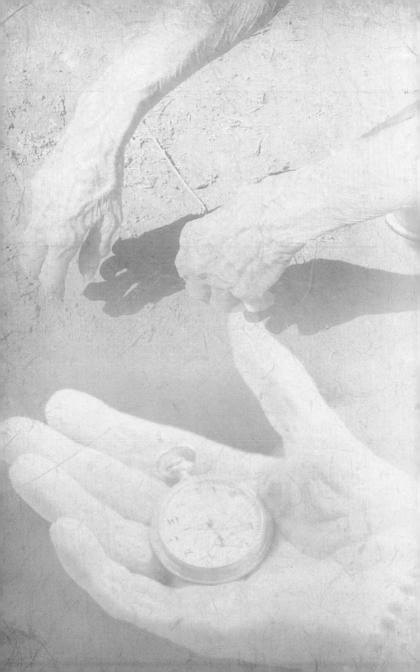

~§ II §~

A Spring Called Heaven

No eye has seen,
no ear has heard,
no mind has conceived
what God has prepared
for those who love him—
but God has revealed it to us by his Spirit.

1 CORINTHIANS 2:9–10

As an adolescent and young adult, I often asked myself, *What is life about? Why was I born? Why do I live?*

Have those questions plagued you, too?

The questions weren't meant to be morbid; I just had an honest desire to make sense of what I observed. I had seen something of the ugliness, sorrows, and sufferings of life and, above all, what seemed to me the futility of it all…with death waiting for everyone at the end. As I saw it, the times of beauty, joy, and richness that I experienced in life did not begin to cancel out the harsh, grinding realities.

What was life all about anyway?

When I was in my early twenties, the day came when the Holy Spirit began to convict my heart of sin—a new word and a new concept to me. At first, I tried to straighten my life out on my own, by my own will, in my own strength. To my amazement, I found I could not!

I could not love God with all of my being; I loved myself more.

I could not love others as I loved myself.

And these were His two great commands! The harder I tried to keep every thought, word, and action absolutely right before God, the more helpless I felt to do those very things.

Somehow, intuitively, I knew that God was holy, and I knew very well that I was not. Nor could I make myself so. Without ever having read it in the pages of a Bible, I knew that I was separated from Him and would be so forever if I couldn't change myself. Then I heard that Christ died for sins—that His blood cleansed from all sin. And yet I still couldn't comprehend how that related to me. Surely I had to at least *try* to make myself acceptable.

A week later, kneeling at my bedside, pounding my fists in anger at God for not helping me be what I must be, I lifted my eyes to the risen Christ and cried out to Him for help.

In that very instant the Word I'd heard rushed back into memory: *"The blood of Christ cleanses from all sin."*

Just that suddenly, I could see.

94

Just that quickly, light flooded every dark corner.

I saw He was the Savior. *My* Savior.

Yes, I was sinful. I could not—could never—make myself good enough for God. But that's why He came! He died to pay the penalty for my sins so that I might be cleansed from them and restored to God. Right then and there, kneeling beside my bed, I asked Him into my life as Lord and Savior. A deep peace flooded my heart.

A week or two later, I was sitting on a bench in Central Park, New York City, nibbling at my sack lunch, throwing crumbs to the pigeons. I had begun taking some lunch hours to be alone and think about this new personal relationship with the Lord. As I sat gazing at the skyscrapers silhouetted against the sky, my eyes followed the lines of those sleek buildings right up into the clear heavens.

Suddenly, for the second time, light dawned.

This time I saw with crystal clarity what life was all about.

In a flash, it all made sense to me.

Heaven is what life was all about!

This life on earth is but preparation—a staging area—for the eternal reality of heaven. He would use all the events in this warped scene of life, from the smallest to the largest, the most pleasurable to the most painful, to prepare me for my place in heaven. Earth was where my faith would be tried, my character formed, and my rewards in heaven established. My rewards—or loss of them—would be eternal. During this life I had the opportunity to advance His kingdom, become more like my Lord, and lay up treasure for that glorious, endless future with Him.

I didn't know yet that God said those very things in His Word, but in that bright noonday sun on a park bench in New York City, He spoke those truths to my heart. He showed me that the troubles and sufferings of this life are actually working *for* me (not against me) to produce an eternal glory in heaven beyond anything my mind could conceive. (See 2 Corinthians 4:17.)

In that same moment, I also saw that this life was as a millisecond compared to the endless years of eternity. I had been blind to these things! That day, at the spring called Heaven, I saw. Life made sense at last. My landscape hadn't changed at all, but it was as though I had a new set of eyes. Under the arid, stony soil of a ruined creation was the vast aquifer of His redeeming love. Out of that love He had died to open heaven's door. Eden was as nothing compared to living with Him in that blazing glory forever.

I was made for Him.

I was made for heaven.

~ 12 ~

SAND IN MY EYES

I will wait for the LORD,
who is hiding his face....
I will put my trust in him.

ISAIAH 8:17

*S*ometimes when the dry wail of wind sweeps over
Death Valley, dust clouds block the sun's light. Sand gets
in my eyes, and I can no longer see the spring called Heaven.

The storms shut out the daylight, and God seems endless
miles away. I see the harsh, stinging evil of the world and the
abrasive, heartbreaking events of life. Doubts loom out of the
darkened landscape, and I find myself questioning His love—
even His very existence.

Is all I've known and experienced simply a product of my imagi-
nation? Why doesn't He explain Himself? Is He really in control? Why
doesn't He DO something about the distortion, casual cruelty, and evil

in the world? Why doesn't He do something NOW?

I long for Him in these dark moments and feel abandoned in a howling wilderness. Try as I might, I can't get the sand out of my eyes to see things differently. To stop groping for Him and accept this darkness is the last thing I want to do. Yet the words He has taught me come drifting back to me through the storm:

"Wait in silence for God only…. Wait in silence for God only…."

Wait?

Yes, once again, He asks me to simply wait. And trust.

Wait in total darkness—no sun, no moon, no stars.

Wait in naked faith, with no other props to cling to.

Wait for the dust storm to cease.

Jesus Christ promises that "he who follows Me shall not walk in darkness, but shall have the light of life." One thing I have learned: The Promiser keeps His promises.

On one occasion, after God blew one of these dust storms away, I opened my eyes to see the Lord Jesus in a new light. For thirty-three years, Jesus walked through the harsh desert of this world. For Him, the wilderness did not sing; the desert did not bloom; the mountains were not made low; the crooked places were not made straight nor the rugged places a plain. He walked through the misery, endured the hatred, experienced the betrayal, bore the injustice, suffered the violence, and tasted the bitterness of death.

His sole resource was God.

Then while on the cross, in the face of death, He was forsaken by the Father and plunged into a black hole of darkness beyond the limits of language to describe. He took my place as one cut off from God. He died to redeem me out of deepest darkness and in resurrection to unite me with Himself forever.

In an infinitesimal way, my experience in those sandstorms—my dark night of feeling forsaken by God—gave me the merest glimpse of what He had suffered for me—the actual abandonment by God! In that moment of fresh understanding, I gained a new confidence that because of His work (all dark-night feelings to the contrary) nothing could ever separate me from God. Seeing how my Lord suffered when He was separated from God, what it cost Him to open heaven's door for me, made Him even more precious to my heart.

Sometimes it is not the dust storm, but the sand that I have allowed to accumulate that hides the spring.

It takes work to dig out the spring.

It takes heaven's perspective to remember that the Death Valley of a world under God's curse will not change until Christ's return.

It takes patience to wait for heaven, where God, the righteous judge, will right all wrongs and explain the mystery of evil.

It takes time to get refocused, to stop drinking the "bad waters."

It takes effort to remind myself that He walks through this harsh world with me, even when I have no sense of it.

ℝ *It takes energy to set my thoughts on heaven, my true home, and to live in its joys in the here and now.*

ℝ *It takes long, thirsty days to remember where the spring pours forth refreshment and the water is always sweet.*

At times the wind-spun eddies of dust dim my vision, and I see the painful events that blow into my life as forces working against me. I feel as though I'm playing the game of life on the Devil's Golf Course. I forget that God intends to turn these very trials into something good, giving me the opportunity to become more like Christ.

I forget that my very response to these hurtful trials and bruising setbacks will determine my place in His kingdom and the extent of my service to the King throughout eternity.

Yes, there is always a certain amount of sand in the air. We are told that there will always be a certain blurred vision until we see the Lord Jesus face-to-face.

Maybe so. But waiting in the dimness is only a brief prelude to reigning in the light.

A Spring Called Beloved

The LORD your God is with you,
he is mighty to save.
He will take great delight in you,
he will quiet you with his love,
he will rejoice over you with singing."

Zephaniah 3:17

As I sat in my lawn chair that day contemplating the spring called Heaven, I realized that needed a second spring to keep the oasis green—a spring for the harsh, personal struggles and perplexities in the here and now.

These were years of conflict on the job...pain in personal relationships... emptiness in my soul.

Lord, this is what I need within me—springs fed by a massive reservoir. Otherwise, how can I keep fresh in the burning heat of life's deserts: the daily grind, the time crunch, the incessant demands, the long treks of drudgery? How can I stay alive and vital in spirit through the dry days, the dull days?

Nothing,
nothing in the universe
can compare with
being unconditionally loved.

It's no use trying to hide it from You, Lord. Your eyes have surveyed every inch of my heart's desert landscape. You've seen the acres of emptiness, heaped with dark rubble. A patchwork of lifeless salt flats. What little waters there are, are "bad waters." I can't run from this fallen world or the "Death Valley" of my own soul. But Lord, I'm so very thirsty. I need a great source of water continually bubbling up to water the soil of my heart.

Some months later, back in the daily routine at home, God used a strange circumstance to answer the need of my heart. As He had done for Abraham's servant Hagar so long ago, He opened my eyes to see a well in the desert—a gushing spring in the midst of hopeless desolation.

A severely depressed woman had come to me for whatever counsel and help I might be able to offer. She was on her way back from an assignment in Asia and would spend a week with me before returning to her home in another part of the country. Her friends and family were deeply concerned. Alarmed. They hoped that, somehow, I might be able to help her sort through the troubling issues of her life.

I tried hard to do just that. Every moment that I wasn't working, I spent with her. I shared the Scripture and every principle I knew. I listened to her by the hour. Our talks went far into the night.

At the end of the week, however, she was no better. In fact, she seemed a great deal worse. Her depression had deepened. Her despair yawned like a bottomless crevasse in the path ahead. All of those hours with me had accomplished precisely nothing.

The morning she was to leave, I woke up with a sinking heaviness. *A lot of good you've done,* I told myself. *You haven't helped this poor woman one iota. She's leaving your home with a heavier heart than when she arrived. Let's be real, Pamela Reeve...what have you EVER done to help anyone? You're of no use—and probably never will be. You are worthless.*

Out of habit more than desire, I picked my daily devotional book off the nightstand. The opening Scripture for that day cut through my gray mood like the sun through parting clouds.

> *"Again, the kingdom of heaven is like a merchant seeking beautiful pearls, who, when he had found one pearl of great price, went and sold all that he had and bought it."*

MATTHEW 13:45–46, NKJV

Immediately, the Lord spoke to my heart. "Hear Me, My daughter. *You are that pearl to Me.* A pearl of great price."

I closed the book, shutting the door to my heart at the same time, unwilling to believe what He was saying. "Me? A pearl of great value? Common river rock is more likely. I have no value at all. I'm worthless." (It wasn't the first time I had said such words.)

I took my guest to the airport for her early morning flight. The drive was mostly silent. I had nothing left to say and felt overwhelmed with a sense of failure. *She came to me for help. She needed someone. And I'm sending her away as empty as when she walked through my front door. What had she found in my home? An oasis—or more wasteland?*

When I got back home, I found a small, neatly-wrapped package, which my guest had left for me on the dining room table. She shouldn't have done that! I told myself. I certainly hadn't earned it! I pulled away the wrapping and opened the little box.

It was a pearl ring—the most beautiful I had ever seen. And it fit me to perfection.

As I slipped the ring onto my finger, the Lord spoke to my heart again. "Say what you will. Imagine what you like. Shut Me out if you can. My gift cannot be earned, only given. Yet I tell you once again, you are a pearl of great price in My eyes. You are My beloved."

His beloved!

This time, I drank it in. This time, I let His words seep into the parched soil of my soul. What refreshing waters began to pour forth from that deep pool in my oasis. I wore the pearl ring day and night for many years. It remains my most precious possession. Each time I look at it, I am reminded, *"You are God's beloved, a pearl of great price. He gave His life to purchase you."*

When feelings of worthlessness steal across my soul like afternoon shadows, I look at the pearl and remind myself, *You are beloved. Yes—you!*

There is nothing more wonderful in time or eternity than to know that you are deeply and perfectly loved. It is sweet, cold water for the deepest thirst of your heart. It is the spring that bubbles up to bring life to your desert. The great inexhaustible aquifer beneath you is the Lord's intense love for you, *just as you are*. He is a never-changing, never-failing source of love.

113

CHOSEN

I am His chosen one.

Why is it so hard—so heartbreakingly difficult at times—to hold on to such a simple truth?

Why do the desert sands blow into the spring and choke its flow?

Why do I have to keep digging and digging to let the stream run free?

For so long I had viewed myself as Death Valley—with its ugliness, its uselessness. That was all I could see. I hadn't seen the beautiful oasis in me, vibrant with life in the midst of it.

It is true; by nature I am a wasteland. I am a fallen being, totally corrupted from what humanity was originally designed to be. But God Himself stepped into my life to redeem me. He came to dwell within me and created an oasis in the deepest part of me, a new life that is pure, clean, and righteous. A life just like His Son's, because it is His Son's.

He delights in that new life within me. He is through with the old; it's dead and buried with Christ in His sight. And He would say to me: "Stop looking at that old life. I have! Look at the you that is so infinitely precious in My sight. Dwell on the fact that I delight in you, My beloved. Stop connecting with your darkness. Connect with the beauty of My risen life within you. You were on My heart eons before I created the galaxies and scattered a trillion suns across the void. I personally designed you and take great pleasure in the work of My hands. I set My love on you before the ages of time. No earthly father has had a fraction of the delight in a long-awaited newborn that your heavenly Father had in you when you stepped into time."

How deeply, unspeakably satisfying to be chosen.

Yes, there are still times when that truth fades from view under the relentless pressure of circumstance, seasons when the windstorms howl and the sands blow in to choke my spring. There are days when I have to dig away the accumulated sand to clear a path for the bubbling waters. And sometimes that is difficult work—especially if I've endured a string of personal failures or a stinging blast of criticism. At other times, it is because I've simply been too busy or have forgotten to remind myself that I'm His cherished beloved.

But as the years go by, the thought wells up more and more consistently, and I say with Solomon's bride, "I am my beloved's, and his desire is for me" (Song of Songs 7:10, NASB).

DESIRED

What a wonder it is to be desired—not for your accomplishments, but for just being you. There is no more refreshing water to the soul. He wants you to know that in the deep places of your heart.

This life, with its inward and outward deserts, is the scene of His wooing. He, my heavenly Bridegroom, invites me to walk through this "Death Valley" on His arm, leaning on Him.

Christ, my Bridegroom, has been my Protector, Comforter, and Helper through many years of single life. Above all, He wants me to know that at any hour of the day or night, no matter what my circumstances, I am deeply and intensely loved.

What a romance is ours! It is tenderly beautiful in the here and now. What it will be in its culmination at the marriage supper of the Lamb is beyond imagination. He calls me to drink continuously at the spring called Beloved, whose waters remind me that I am chosen, precious, and dearly loved.

Meanwhile, I have found the Lord so very patient with me as we walk through the dry lands together. While I have been planning for now, He has been planning for heaven. And sometimes, when the wind is still, I hear again His tender whisper:

"Remember heaven, Beloved. We're on our way to a wedding."

*In the harsh desert,
the Bridegroom woos.*

WILDERNESS MEMORIES

For the LORD your God
is bringing you into a good land—
a land with streams and pools of water,
with springs flowing in the valleys and hills;
a land with wheat and barley, vines and fig trees,
pomegranates, olive oil and honey;
a land where bread will not be scarce
and you will lack nothing.

DEUTERONOMY 8:7–9

For long years now, there have been few deserts on my journey. My trail has often led through deep, cool forests. I have paused to gaze at shy, delicate wildflowers and to stand near the thunder of rainbow-wreathed waterfalls.

Yes, there have been some deep gorges along the way, but they have often led to sunny, flower-carpeted meadows. There have been steep ascents with hairpin switchbacks, but the views from high above timberline have been well worth the climb. A sharp eye must watch for the deadly rattlesnake, but it can also catch sight of the high-soaring eagles.

My heart is light.

Joyously so.

I have survived the deserts, passed through them, and learned again and again that whatever the stretch of trail ahead, my Father has good purposes and ample provisions for the journey. What peace of mind!

The realization that my High Priest walks the trail at my side has never left me. What an ever-present support He is! Together, with great joy, we approach the throne of grace where I present my petitions, worship, and adore. What rest of heart!

I look forward to heaven with great anticipation. Heaven…where our hearts will pour forth pure worship. Heaven…where with vastly heightened abilities we will engage in God the Creator's ever expanding purposes.

The darkness, gloom, and sorrow of this world—a world estranged from God—remain. I long for the new heavens and the new earth, where "there shall no longer be any mourning or crying or pain. Broken lives surround me. I grieve for them—deeply. I yearn for the day that "God shall wipe away every tear from their eyes." Even so, my heart lives in heaven. Eternal life has already begun. In the glory of the Father's home, my heavenly Bridegroom, who wooed me in the desert, watches and waits for me. Amid the songs of angels, He hears my footfalls drawing ever nearer. Soon, and very soon, we will meet face-to-face. Anticipation of that moment reminds me…I do not walk toward sunset and gathering darkness; I walk toward sunrise and eternal day.